Space Cake Amsterdam

THE PINT
Heineken

NIRALA SERIES

Space Cake Amsterdam

& Other Poems from Europe and America

YUYUTSU RD SHARMA

NIRALA

Nirala Publications
G.P.O. Box 7004
Daryaganj, New Delhi-110002
niralabooks@yahoo.co.in
www.niralapublications.com

ISBN-81-8250-059-1

First Edition 2010 by Howling Dog Press, Colorado

Indian Edition: in Nirala Series: 2014

Cover and Book Design : S.A.A. Wasti

Cover Illustrations: Aixia de Villanova & Yuyutsu Sharma

Inside Illustrations: Fran and Yuyutsu Sharma

Acknowledgements

Gratitude is expressed to the editors and publishers of the magazine, journals and anthologies where some of these poems were published:
"London Bombing," *The World Record* Edited by Neil Ashley & Anna Selby
"De Zwarte Ruiter Cafe" *Amsterdam Weekly*
"Temple, London" *Pratik Special British Issue*
"Celtic light: Leslie Castle", "Look-alike, Galway" *Annapurna Poems,* Nirala Publications
"Song of the Small Stalls," *Special Immigrant Indian Writers' Issue* and "Mules on the Tube," *Exiled Ink,* London,
"Ruigoort" *Ruigoort Anthology*, Amsterdam,
"Cleveland" *Rattapallax,* New York
"At forty you die.." *The City Poetry,* Cleveland

Printed at
Jaico Printers
New Delhi-110002

Praise for
Yuyutsu RD Sharma's works

'Yuyutsu Sharma's new collection is concerned with notions of home and being away in the exotic elsewhere. Home strikes deep, like 'my grandma / asleep // on a plump / bubble // of a folk song' but is then flung into the great proper nouns of New York, all detail, all observation and dazzle. The poems are registered at the tips of the eyes then connected with the sense of deep home. That is where the power lies. It emerges through ear and mouth as a kind of cosmopolitan love letter.'
George Szirtes
British Poet, winner of Faber Memorial Prize & T.S. Eliot Prize

'Yuyutsu Sharma, a Himalayan poet who studied his craft in the United States and on the mule paths of high Himalayas has brought a visionary sensibility to his New York poems. They read like Federico Garcia Lorca having a Hindu dream, or like Allen Ginsberg risen from the dead and howling out a peyote vision for 2013. Their ambition, like Lorca's in his Poet in New York or like Hart Crane's in his New York epic, The Bridge, is to write an epic vision of the city--and ultimately of America--in linked lyrics. Here are the Twin Towers flaming like the red tongue of Kali, goddess of destruction, a city like a yellow-eyed demon, Hurricane Sandy burrowing into the island's groin like a furious porcupine. Sharma is "a shaman...black bag bulging / from magical rainbows, / serpents from an Hindu Heaven, / skull of an abducted female Yeti," and he casts spells in these strange, visionary, outrageous and magical poems.'
Tony Barnstone
The Albert Upton Professor and Chair of English
Whittier College, Author/Translator of Everyman's Chinese Erotic Poems

If Langston Hughes, Federico García Lorca and Frank O'Hara were exhumed to rub their recollections of New York City together over dal and black tea, they might produce a manuscript as rapturous as Yuyutsu Sharma's love letter to the five boroughs. Infused with the mythology of Sufi saints and Hindu deities, Blizzard Go Delhi is nonetheless utterly contemporary, juxtaposing Duane Reedes and Occupy Wall Streeters alongside Punjabi wheat fields and muscular Halwai-confectioners working over huge cauldrons of oil. Unrepentant in its sensuality, self-assured and visionary, Sharma's book is an extravagant tour de force that shows us that stepping off the train into New York City is to enter a realm "of wandering winter spirits and wavering speeches...a bedlam vision of a bedroom utopia that tries very hard every night to find a partner of sleep." Tries, but thankfully for us, fails and instead stays up to channel the manic, long-limbed energy of the city in this memorable and original verbal jazz solo. This book is a poetic triumph.
-Ravi Shankar, Executive Director of *Drunken Boat*, author of seven books/ chapbooks of poetry & co-editor of *W.W. Norton & Co.'s Language for a New Century: Contemporary Poetry from Asia, the Middle East & Beyond*

"A Blizzard in My Bones," Yuyu's deeply moving new collection and a remarkable addition to modern urban literature. It is Nepal and Hinduism and Brooklyn and Manhattan and Greenwich Village drawn together in a new Space Cake: Amsterdam; but here the hallucinogen-stoked celebration is amid the concrete and steel heights of Metropolis.
David Austell, Professor, NYU, Author of Little Creek and Other Poems

Capacious and wild, offering itself energetically to contrasting continents and sensibilities, Sharma's ambitious and honest New York collection offers a vivid tribute to Lorca, its presiding muse.
Annie Finch, winner of Robert Fitzgerald Award and author of *Spells: New and Selected Poems.*

Each poem is a delight in itself, a discovery, a new turn of phrase, a new sensation, a world of sound and light, and visions all colliding against each other to provide an unexpected and haunting experience.
David Clark in *Exiled Ink,* London

Yuyutsu RD lives close to Everest. His poetry climbs mountains, swims in rivers and paints the falling leaves in copper. This tango with nature also occurs when Yuyutsu RD closes the window for a moment...
Ronny Someck in *Iton77,* Tel Aviv

The poems... are shining jewels of passion, energy and splendid craft, redolent with vivid, dreamlike visual imagery, strengthened by realistic observation and powered by strong male eroticism. His is an unabashed return to the male gaze that is refreshing and solemn by turns, reminding one of the stirring sounds of rolling drums and beating rain...
Sucheta Das Gupta in *The Himalayan Times,* Kathmandu

A fiercely sublime poet ...the book confirms an enormous talent, as well as purity of purpose with which he approaches his calling. Lines jump out, burning themselves into your consciousness.
Eddie Woods in *Amsterdam Weekly*

With this buoyantly audacious work, Yuyutsu RD should be assured of his place in the canon of Asian poetry.
In this new volume he conveys the people and places, the flora and fauna of the Annapurna area of Nepal with an exhilaratingly fresh vision. It is poetry where pastoral elegy becomes fused with magic realism; where earthy common-sense mysticism becomes interlaced with a lush sexuality. The book is a voluptuous and loving evocation of Nepal and I admire its dramatic intensity.
Cathal O Searcaigh, Ireland

Yuyutsu RD Sharma has his feet firmly planted on the ground. His poetry is rooted in its landscape and environment and thereby gains its strength. He has also served the muse assiduously over the decades and small wonder that she has rewarded him.
— **Keki N. Daruwala,** *New Delhi*

Yuyutsu RD Sharma's poetry runs clear, tender, and passionate with a rage that often erupts volcanic in the face of the cruelty, despair, and

injustice that saddles the disenfranchised poor of the earth. Poems powerful and devastating, yet gentle as flower petals wafting to earth in a summer breeze.
Michael Annis, senior editor, *Howling Dog Press,* Colorado

"Something is always happening in Yuyutsu's poetry. Like some burning concern for truth, something that, I think, a poem should do. For this, we owe Yuyutsu much.
— **Jayanta Mahapatra,** Cuttack, India
Yuyutsu's poetry touches on concerns of global matters, acknowledging that we can never with violence create a Utopia or "construct a gorgeous pagoda from/furious flames/and whistling winds ... Such lines capture for me the futility of the Iraq War, which I refuse to dignify with its official title, even more euphemistic and tainted with doublethink than earlier misadventures. We can't build even a humble pagoda from furious flames and whistling winds.
— **David Ray,** The United States of America

"Yuyutsu R.D. brings to the Indian readers a distinct flavor of the Nepalese landscape and culture, in a sequence of poems that pulsate with needle-sharp images—Equally sensitive is his language that, scrupulously avoids stilted diction-words or phrases. His writing is so densely imagistic that he holds reader's attention all the way through. Behind plethora of packed images is a genuine concern for the human predicament—the trials and tribulations of the destitute everywhere. Hunger is the theme that runs as an under current-hunger that gnaws into the vitals of both humans and animals."
—**Shiv K. Kumar** in *The Hindustan Times*

Yuyutsu has a good eye and a good ear:
The rain stopped in the jungle.
The cicada stopped its chirr.
To have an ear for a sudden silence in unique.
—*The Hindustan Times*

"Yuyutsu's poetry has long been a part of the Nepalese consciousness: we use his more aphoristic lines as a paradigm of contemporary Nepali political and social changes."
--*The Kathmandu Post*

This is what **Asiaweek** has to say of **Yuyutsu's translations of Nepali poetry:**
'... magnificent achievement evoking lives of Nepalese peasants while remaining highly readable... The reader will come away breathless from these short, wonderfully concentrated poems'

These vivid and readable translations show the poets coming to terms both with political development and with the influence of Western modernism in literature.
— Allen W. Thrasher,
Library of Congress, Washington DC

NIRALA SERIES 7

Contents

PART ONE

Wind Islands

Temple, London

for Maggie Hindley

Wind howled
like the trumpet of a fierce Kali
rushed in through
the Temple Tube Station
to slap my face
to smother the flame
of my breath
and blind my vision
as I soared
floaing up the steely slope
of the ecsclators
in spirit of reaching
a hillside shrine
that our goddesses
always prefer to live on.

Once up
out of the Station
in the freezing cold
as I exerted to push
my overcoat up
my shaking frame
I saw her there
on the wet pavement
out alone in the open
with a swollen black eye
and an issue of *The Big Issue*
held like a trophy,
a sacrificial rooster
against her sagging breast.

Someone left a pen...

On the forsaken
table of a restaurant, Zwarte Ruiter,
Starbucks, Willy's Bar,
someone left a pen for me.

Someone left
a feather, a note scribbled
in a language illegible
along the stony pavements of a dome,
Milan, Rome, Koln.

Someone left a page,
flash of a naked conch shell on an abandoned shore,
Den Haag, Bremenhaven, Southampton.

Someone waited for me
at night in the garden on a white bench naked,
naked like a white cat
facing the listless sheen of a green pond.

Someone left an email address,
a card, a name on a scrap of paper
in a city bus, or anguish
on the screeching brakes of an underground train.

Someone kissed my dark eyes
in sleep as she laid her silvery head
on my shoulder, a book in her hand –
midsummer night's dream.

Someone left warmth
of a Sun from her lungs,
a warm mouth, zaika of a scented tongue,
Dutch, Deutsch, English, French.

Someone offered a bottle of wine,
a cigarette, twig of cannabis,
pod of a familiar fragrance
aroma of a forgotten paradise,
whiff of wet warmth of a burning bush.

Someone left a pen
on the palpable table of my travels

I leaned
to pick it up

and place it
in the black bag of my memory.

Confusion

Your soft touch
wrote the story.

The waves
of your golden hair
that I kept holding back,
tucking them
behind your ears,
like North Sea
combing shores of Den Haag

Would you hire me,
I asked,
for a life time
to keep them in order?

"I would chop them off"
you replied,
"and stay clear of confusion."

In Europe

We learnt to
French-kiss in Europe,
discovered secret
chambers of our bodies
musk of the hidden hues of lust
your breasts, my chest
your round moons, my line running straight
up to kiss the sovereign summits of bliss.

We learnt to shed clothes
in the temples of our flesh,
learnt to make love naked in Europe,
earned the prizes, the black berry,
rose tips, crimson doorways,
my eloquent pen thrumming
the other mouth of your body.

Wind

On this island
Wind wakes me from a lifetime's sleep.

Wind. wind wind.

Wind shakes me
off my balance, rattling

the Empire's python poise
that for decades I'd taken for granted.

What is it? I ask
a song of the living waters?

Is it the fire
that fed his potent pen

the tempest
that fanned the funnel beneath his magic cauldron?

Or the third traveller
that walked beside Krishna and Christ?

Wind. wind. wind.
Wind that stalks over

the rock of my chest
like a furious Kali.

Wind. wind.wind.

Wind that wrenches morsels
of sleep from my eyes, a furious hound

that makes me limp
from the terror of its murderous grip.

Wind that in the middle
of a lonely night thumps like a Yeti

over our rooftop,
rushes in through window cracks

to hit my headpiece
Wind. wind. wind.

A gale that turns brutal
and screams and rakes the skeletons of history,

a rainstorm that lunges
at the pillaged museums of an apologetic sky

a brutal sexist
that strips everything bare

a serial killer
dropping young maples naked in the public parks.

Wind. wind. wind.
What is it? I ask.

Is it a demon,
some general Dyer's ruthless eyes?

Is it the power wind
that visits the mighty island where the Sun never sets?

Or a singing Sufi saint
begotten like my own late father

of a divine frenzy, dancing
like its master and the maker?

A nomadic wind
that throbs in my dreams

like a fluttering fish
of a forgotten anger, protruding

from his crazed forehead
as he appears again once again

in a Siddhartha moment
waving his farewell to us

to join caravans of the ashen ascetics
and wandering winds of the world.

London Bombings

I didn't desert the Underground
to join the British waterways
or party on the shores of the Northern Sea.

I didn't leave the streets,
Oxford, Piccadilly, Marylebone High Street,
to go into the lonely Room
to read Bronte, Bill or Da Vinci.

I didn't desert the West End
to go for meadows dotted with sheep.

I moved like William Blake
in the double-decker buses
deciphering terror alphabets
of a script of hidden sleep.

Nottinghill, Tooting, Camden,
Fullham, Wembley, Hammersmith,
I stayed on to join
carnivals of primal ecstasy.

I was there when they brought
their forgotten gods and demons out from their skins.
I fell in love with her
as Elizabeth got drunk and kept swearing,
smearing her purple lipstick
with shaking long fingers all over her mouth

Sitting in her lover's lap,
she kept calling me 'husband':
Husband! Husband!
as her teenage daughter
opposite us lay in waiting.

I was there when they celebrated
the death of Jane's family
and their charade of being
proverbial husband/wife went on
like a morality play
faming the last shame humanity's grandmothers.

It was there that Elizabeth's body
glowed like a hillside hearth in a room where
a statue of the wooden
Krishna broke into a smile.

"Put your Hinduish/Buddhist marks on your forehead
or wear pendants showing your holy gods,
you could be taken as a terrorist
and shot five times in the brain..."
But I refused to desert the square
littered with blotches of the dark ink of terror...
I didn't desert the squares of the mighty Pound
to cry secretly in the nearby towns where
under common ground Marx and Freud lay buried....

I moved about fearlessly
under the shadow of Marble Arch
kissed her beneath
the tall column of Trafalgar Square.
and entered immaculate doors
of New Age goddess on the swelling Thames' banks,
daring to risk the Empire's familiar hand,
Prospero's mighty magic wand.

A Visit to Bristol

A visit to Bristol
would make you about a century older...

At the wide quay
icy rainstorms would shake
you off your balance, tearing
your umbrellas into tatters.
From the parched throat
of the famed lion
you would hear sighs
and stifled groans for the waters
that've dried over the decades.
A local gentleman would slyly
leave open the door of the toilet
facing your free sofa at The Coffee Republic.
Then and there would you
learn your shame of being a Gandhi.
You would start hearing muffled cries
of the captives piercing skies
of new found lands, cages
reeking of human feces
and goat-urine and tears
of slime dripping like black tar
from just God's own eyes.
You would hear the thud
of a nail being stuck
in someone's head at St. Nicholas' market.
You would imagine a human head cut
and stuck like a trademark
or a trophy on someone's polished ivory door.
"Yesser, we do deal...."
You would see a flash of light
in the ancient mariner's eye,
his heart pouring rivers of darkness.

Even old Naptune's trident
of blunt blades wouldn't
guard guilt of your skies.
Mr. Kurtz, he's dead...
Only at the Slow Food Market
Hardyfolks would resume
their old roles and resort to
the oldest trade of the land
at the very doorsteps of SuperSainsburies –
Sussex turkey, Thaw mulled wine,
Brown cows organic, Gloucestershire cheese,
York's homemade minced pies...

A visit to Bristol would
teach you to count time
or your own life
as steps on a stairway
ending in an abyss --
one two, ten, twenty,
thirty, forty, one two

A visit to Bristol would
make you about a century older...

Strokestown, Famine Museum

Daffodils have sprung
along the Castle's crumbling walls,
jaundiced faces' floral reincarnations.

Jar of leeches in the regal kitchen is empty.
Outside the horses graze
on green meadows shaking manes
rising and falling like opaque sails
that once carried coffin-ships
across the stretch of the parched tongue of Atlantic.

Pitcher of blood has burst
into a sunrise along the Celtic shores.

Bullets that shot the landlord
of dubious Mortellos erected
to save/cage/calm cries of the famished
lie rusting, brittle and wintry.

Was he St. Kavin,
parrots aflutter on his humble shoulders?

Or ugly Gulliver picking
handful of pygmies and hurling them
towards the ferries
afloat on the black sea waters?

Strangely the town reminds me
of funeral grounds where mutilated limbs
of the warriors slain
in the Mahabharata were shoved
into a colossal pile
and put aflame to perform frugal cremation rites.

Muse:Two Fragments

1.

Loose Muse, Dublin

On the last leg
of my travels in Europe

at Dublin airport
I finally found her,

this dazzling blonde
of sandalwood limbs

naturel looks, porcelain skin,
arched eyebrows, sweeping eyeliners, succulent chin

sitting atop a low stool
opposite the blitz of the duty-free shopping malls

right beneath
the euro clock ticking in the plush passageways

to eke out
an austere living and a flaccid tatter of sunlight

this curvy muse that I'd desired to meet
in the desperate hours of my lonely knight journeys

a busty goddess that if
I were a priest, I'd have placed her in a shrine

a nimble-footed nymph
who probably had been the Queen of Egypt in her past life

in the aftermath
of the past century's vague and fretful orgasm

sitting in slime
of post-post conquests, a failed female yeti

on a shoe-shine stool
facing high-backed mahogany chairs

embellished from the mocking tails
of Celtic tigers and shame of drowned bogmen's skins

in silence shining shoes
of the ugliest man in the world.

2.

Book of Happiness: London

On the Northern line
in the brightly lit bogie

opposite me
oblivious of the sliding doors

opening onto
the escalators and the neon *Way Outs*

rabbit nosed, soft
and white, barely able

to carry her tiny purple bags
hanging beneath her bemused eyes

full of cargos
of the worries of the whole world

this young girl
the same age as my daughter

reading
paperback edition of the book--

How We
Choose To Be Happy.

De Zwarte Ruiter Cafe

They treated me like
a drunken lorry driver would

a nubile girl
from a remote Himalayan village.

"Can you call the dead,
you man from the Himalayas?" one of them hollered.

Raising her voice above the rocking music
in the cafe, other shouted, "Nonsense! Pure bullshit!"

"Look here, answer!" the former insisted,
"Can you stop my late Grandpa

from visiting my bedroom twice a month."

She held her friend's hand
to stop her from offering me a handshake

and raised her sleeveless plump arm
in the air as if holding a dagger

"Whooooo!" she cried, "I switch off the light
and whooooo! there it comes-- Whoooooo!

Can you tell me if the dead
can come back to disturb your peace?

Can you explain why I dream of crocodiles
with baby faces chasing me

as I run miles and miles
of bleeding river's expanse ?

You man from the land of Yeti,"
she picked up her empty wine glass

and laying it beside
an ashtray started naming objects.

"Okay, let's say this is my grandpa, the dead one,
but tell me, can he come back to visit me in my bedroom?

Do they exist,
these silent travellers of our disturbed sleep?"

Two young women of Den Haag kissed like lovers
and asked--"What does your Buddha say about this?"

They giggled and then a silence spread.
I knew they wished me to wear

a shaman's feathered crown for my head
and dance round and round for several centuries

to avenge the atrocities of the male Buddhas
in the corridors of history for them.

Gentleman, Van Gogh's museum

After a tempestuous night in bed
she took me to Vincent Van Gogh's museum,

ravens coming over golden wheat fields,
his wintry Dutch face
blowing up million dykes of sanity, screeching pain
pouring out from his bandaged easels,
bleeding ears of his sullen brush
loaf of bread that'd grown stale and smelly
in my own hometown, small rickety chairs
and a round mahogany table in a shady pub
on an anonymous Paris street,
blood rushing out of blazing sunflowers
wearing colors of my mother's dreams
before her death.

Like an ill omen
a black bird flew over my moist eyes
pecked at the pod of her womb
and left a tear in her uterus
that in the later years made the stalk
of her dandelion bend inelegantly.

Wasn't it my fault, the haste
with which I wriggled out of her slithering tube
to face the blinding bulb
of blood over my Punjabi wheat fields?

Mama! I held her bent body
and kissing her broad forehead in my mind
left in a huff
slamming the heavy museum door on her...

Later in the souvenir shop,

she lay her golden head
over my shaking shoulders

and shyly said,
"You know, you aren't a gentleman!"

Dublin: Bog man's Tongue

for Mark Leslie

Lord Mayor's Spire
of stainless steel rises amidst speechless monuments of stone.

I rush up
and down the Moor Street

looking for someone
who resembles Yeats

O' Neil or Seamus Heaney
or speaks Gaelic like my own Cathal Ó Searcaigh.

I walk the streets
Ó Connell, Parnell or Henry

thread through
Georgian squares with blind-eyed windows

cross over the Irish bridge
over the dark river Liffy

past Trinity
up the Grafton street

to find some Ulysses
dozing in a Bleeding Horse's bar.

Or Joyce himself
walking with his stick

towards the Grisham Hotel
to raise souls of the dead or to chat with gold-toothed ladies...

I look for garrulous men
and chattering women straight from the plays of Synge.

I seek out the stories
of forgotten Gandhi in the alleys of Dublin castle.

Celtic tiger fumes
with a twisted tongue in the blitz of its supermarkets,

its sister Dart
snakes along the parks of pleasure

where once Oscar Wilde lay
shivering and cold and penniless.

Like Shiva's serpent
it circles round blue Sea's neck.

The city's crab legs
thump the waters in joy

as finally a bright Sun comes out
to mock the myth of the incessant Irish downpours.

Only drowned bog man's
rubbery body bag put on show in the city centre

speaks Gaelic and reads
the Book of Kells like Bhagwat Gita.

Celtic light: Leslie Castle

After a while
little flustered by my pagan adulation

she blushed,
her cheekbones blazed

like Annapurna summits
in the ruddy light of the morning sun,

her nose twitched
and she pleaded,

almost on
the edge of an accusation:

"If you won't stop
taking my photos,

I'd start
shining your shoes."

Her face glowed from
the shimmer of the tiny lake

slumbering outside
her castle window in the early hours of the night.

Inside, in the hushed
Edwardian silence lit by the aromatic candles

I imagined
a goddess bending onto

the steps of a rock mountain
shining syllables of nomadic winds

and bog lands
with her long tongue and warm breath

fermented from
Celtic coal buried beneath

weight
of centuries of black sleep.

Look-alike, Galway

She held my book
like she would have cradled my baby

had we met and
married in early eighties

and sang songs
of the drifting winds that once visited

her frenzied dance
on the chest of naked glaciers and sun parched continents.

Later in the bar as I stretched
folds of her skin back on her luscious face

years receded into
the faint drawers of my age,

time stepped down
the ladder of my lifespan,

a monkey-thief
in my youth's backyard.

Her long jawed-face
reminded me of Tara

or some rock goddess
as the dark pelt waters from distant bog lands

rushed through
my tumultuous frame.

The moist mouth
in her long Yeti face,

an Irish water well
I tried to see my tiger shadow in ...

"You look like a lover," she said
"I had in the Himalayas decades ago."

PART TWO

Space Cake, Amsterdam

Ruigoord

Artists' village, Amsterdam

We dance
by the Northern Sea, naked.

Each minute
of the day we dance.

Seven days of the week
we dance naked by the Sea.

Twelve months of the year
we dance with nothing on

except joy
of our afterlives.

We dance
without the clothes we wore all our lives,

threadbare webs
of the great Grand Spider.

We dance like the eagles
of the Amazon, snow leopard

pouncing in ecstasy
by the wild edge of turquoise lake

or horses
of Mongolia racing in the Sun.

Our bodies shine
like Indian children dancing

in summer Rain.

Frankfurt

Freckled shell of God's city
turns out to be soft meat of a Donar.

I wipe myself clean
of the dust of miracles that I've carried
like a bird across the oceans.

"Having travelled so far
what difference you think there remains
between fiction and reality,
between shell and kernel?"
says George as his girlfriend blows
her cute nose unabashedly in my presence.

Sex shops, gay salons, Eros,
the nude sculptures in the balcony,
orgies in the underground metro stations,
orgasms in the station toilets,
pointed tip of the blunt Turkish knife
on the soft throat of a newcomer.

In the square next to EU Commercial Centre
an artist draws his penny painting on the pavement
or a singer kicking his heels
at the top of his voice gets just a whistle
from a teenage girl, not sale of his CD.

Walking on the heels of hunger
he knows not it's an obsession here
to polish everything clean, including syllables
of survival he has picked up in this land
of chilled anger where once a man walked like a demigod
where once he dug graves for the living
where once he furled a fetid flag familiar

and fluttering unashamedly in my own land today.

In the chilled air I walk on the stony sidewalks
only to see my own shadow reflected
on the glassy walls of skyscrapers.
But Judith's soft voice touches the tail
of the horse where once a Buddha lived.
A touch of autumn
I've left behind in my own Annapurnas.

George sits home waiting for Susanna like a housewife.
Obediently he shops in the supermarkets, weighing
each penny like a grandma. He feeds the recycle machine
empty bottles to get a euro in return.
I start speaking a language of husbands
that I've mastered on the ghats of Ganges,
a secret invective, an uncanny repartee of bandits..
Judith's face keeps flaring
like silvery peaks of Annapurnas,
fishtail of her golden head bobbing
like a halo of lust denied to humans.

Heidelberg, Danke!

for Christopher Emmrich

The lions that showed their evil
tongues like Durga's,
fire-spitting and fiendish.
Parrots that flew out
of the zoo to dig holes
in the city's concrete to sing
Aha! a song of survival!
to celebrate an eternal spring
beneath valor of vanquished warriors.
River Necktar shines
slithering like a python
round city's robust body.
Why did you delay so much?
Where were you all these years?
How many Christmases did you miss?
You growl like a large ape
without cheekbones.
How much sweat did
you sprinkle over the wounds
roving on the edge of agony
along the mule paths
in the deepest gorges of hunger?
The warm smell of the Christmas Gluhwein
along the University Square in the air
and the lovers kissing
on the bridge above
blue river waters blinding your eyes.
Halfway up the stairway
in the Castle leading you to
the history of a century of Romantic glory
you panic like a child –
Is it worth it, you ask,
this journey into dark glory

of unknown continents?
Scurrying down the slope of the hill
you reach a market place where
a mule opens its mouth of hunger wide
to a child holding a blood-red carrot
for a family snapshot-- Danke!

Mona Lisa's Drunk

Mona Lisa's drunk
from the jasmine scent of her secret fish
drunk from
the magic fruit of her sex,
drunk and stoned
from reveries of hi-tech city's space cakes.

Mona Lisa's drunk
from her green eyes' glamour
that open and kiss
quivering doors of the temple of my face.

Her skirt swirls
in the cold colorless skies of Europe.

Her mysterious smile,
a succulent ploy, demanding
forbidden touch on the crimson Cut
that denies and even divides the divine.

I mildly tug at her scarlet scarf,
wrapping it round my neck, dance,
holding her slender waist
along the shores of Northern Sea flooded
at this hour from goods
and god men from Asia.

Stars above speak
of a vanquished history of sails
eloquent as
Leonardo Da Vinci's brush.

It's here somewhere one time

mandalas of my defeats were drawn.
Along these shores Alexander's horses laughed
and leered before beginning that sojourn into the heart of darkness.
Along these blue waters
I smell the gunpowder that once burst
the chest
of the Continent into blood-soaked fragments.

Years before my birth
it's here somewhere that captors
of Mona Lisa
wrote her ambiguity and my future.

Today she's drunk.
She drools over psychedelic visions of LSD and Ecstasy
spinning mysteriously
like a supernova in the embrace of infested stars.

"I live in a car," she confides.
"I live on the blade of this city's screaming sirens.
I survive on the endless night
in a squatted artists' bar.
I dance on full moon's face
all through the night's eternal orgasm
till I melt and become one -- cup and the bar.
My lips purple blue,
my eyes swollen like Aristophanes' frogs,
blade of my sleek tongue,
my long leathery fish in my mouth
reeking of *sulfa* and exhausted sea shores.
I burgeon on the Hippie smoke of Sixties.
Spiritualists, Swamis and Surrealists have
masturbated white lotus of my slender body.
Dadaists and Beatles have sucked
salt of my soul for decades.
Buddhists have licked me clean
like stone pillow under sleeping Siddhartha's neck.

Avant - Gardes have lain at my bed for years.
The Punk I taught flowers have fire in them.
I've been traveling now for decades
I've been to Amazon and Americas.
I've been on the Asian loop:
Cambodia, Laos, Vietnam,
Thailand, India, China.
I've plans to visit Tibet,
Kathmandu, Kandahar, Kabul, Kashmir.

She tosses her pink cap onto my head
and taking a sip of red wine from my cup
bends to kiss my dark eyes.
"It's your turn now,
Yu Yu, you man from Asia,
any moment I can pull a blanket
from my car and spreading it
like bejeweled sky
can go into a Tantric trance.

And maybe, maybe,
maybe tonight make love to you
on currents of Euro's swelling tide."

The Ship of Fools

Long sleek blade of the windmill
moved with a snail's speed
in the murky Dutch sky
as Tango ticked in her small car
like the terror needle
of time and odor of lust
from her last night with
her lover from the school days
hit my nostrils.

Mock dramatically, she pulled
tip of her long finger
into her Mona Lisa nose
to distract my gaze on
the museum of her white face,
imploring guilt or betrayal
of my passions

Then near the Canal
across the Munt before
getting out of her car,
she rolled a cannabis joint,
put on her feather fangled black hat
and in a busy street corner
finding a lonely guitarist plucking
in ecstasy started a dance
After a while, turned,
"Hey, don't you forget
to remind me, later in the evening
we've to go to the party
at the Ship of Fools."

Window Dolls

In the lanes
of Noordeinde, Den Haag

it's the window dolls
that you would see everywhere

like idols
of eighty-four thousand Hindu gods

on the streets
of Varanasi or Kathmandu.

And everywhere dogs
trotting along humans

like lusts frozen
along the lonely evenings on the leash.

And taking them to be
the idols in the shrine

I sometime bow to them
fearing their prowess and prime.

Amsterdam, First Descent

Outside Centrum
on a wet, wintry cobblestone street

near Sex Museum
it came thumping its misshapen feet,

its claws dripping blood
its cry ancient, sucking hungers

of the raging sea
on the edge of an inferno...

One-eyed ghost white
blond woman with baggy breasts

tugged at him,
a black man in chains, a fury on a leash...

Before Central square
before Madame Tussauds

before I stepped on
the flaming loop of the concentric canals

shrinking into
a tapering hole of a mandala of lust

I learnt
first lesson

of my descent
into the netherworld of the Northern Sea.

Tours De Wallen

with Eddie Woods

"Eddie had an apartment
in the area once," Sylvie announces
before we begin the tour
of the District the Dutch seemed
proud to possess.
We saunter along the Zeedijk,
pass through Nieuwmarkt and enter
a cobblestone street expecting
blinding sheen of marble limbed
window dolls any moment.
"This is where Camus begins his *La Chute,*
where the main character takes his fall."
Eddie pronounces in his thick New York accent,
almost a Charon on our river of flesh.
And to my question, what happened
to the apartment he had in the District,
he retorts raucously, "Shit happens, Man,
shit happens in life." Then by
the white little chapel in narrow
damp street where red lights
begin to show up, almost tickling
the soul beneath my taut skin,
I hear a mild thud
of a strange silence crashing
like a bubble of Buddhist despondency
over deep sleep
of our Lord in the attic,
a silence that wallops against
nagging skies of flesh
in the corridors of conscience
before the brutal bargain begins.

Space Cake, Amsterdam

"Don't panic," they said,
remain cool like your Krishna,
meditate maybe like Buddha,
uttering 'Om Mani Padme,' the jewel in the lotus,
or lie down and relax
like Vishnu on the python-bed
to float on the ocean's currents,
buoyant on the invisible thread
of your breath in slow motion...

Millions of cats prowled around me.
Smoke from shared sex
and hashish joints stung my eyes.
Unsettling tongue
of an awkward fire fed my stomach.
I skidded queasily towards
a formidable edge,
unknown ominous frontiers of human life...

They laughed a secret laugh
behind my back – "Isn't it crazy that
this man from Kathmandu should get stoned
from a piece of space cake in Amsterdam?"

"Don't be serious, laugh,
celebrate the flame of life!" a woman's voice said.
"Hold my hand; I can imagine
you are alone on this trail.
I'v been there once," she whispered.
Her tongue curled like a dry leaf in my ear
and crackled "How much did you take,
just a piece? I took thirty-eight grams once,
It can be crazy if you don't know it's coming.
Just don't worry too much.

Don't lose your control over things.
You can kiss me if you like,
You can pat my back,
tickle my belly or stroke my breasts
for a while, if it comforts you.
Sometimes it can be heavenly,
this licking the rim of the forbidden frontiers of human life.

"That's what he wants, that's exactly
what he's looking for," a voice leered far off.
"But I have to go ultimately,
I've a man waiting at home for me."

"Maybe read a poem of yours,"
someone said. My heart raced wild
and I heard some-girls gossip in the next room—
What if he gets sick in Europe?
Don't we get sick in Asia?

"Just take it easy," another voice echoed
"You won't go psychotic. Remember one thing,
whatever happens, you can always make a comeback."

Faces of my dear ones veered past my face.
I felt delicate thread of my life
slipping through my fingers

"Hey man, it's fine. Don't worry too much."
My host shouted. "Drink lots of water."
Drink black tea or coffee," a guest suggested.
"or take lots of orange juice."
"Maybe sing your favorite song," a woman said.
"Or recite one of your Hindu mantras."
"Maybe stick your finger into your throat"
another voice came sheepishly, "And throw up.
You probably haven't digested everything yet."

Questions came like wind slaps.
"Can you tell me what they call boredom
in your mother tongue? Do you remember
your email account and password?
Discuss your children, if you have any.
Shall I bring my little daughter before you?
Maybe you'd feel better then,
seeing her brilliant eyes."

I imagined a child's face and clung to it,
like a penitent would hold onto
a sacred cow's tail in his afterlife,
and slept on it, all through the river of blood...

Hours passed by
and then I heard someone say—
What if he had freaked out?
What if Death had stalked our house tonight?

Hearing these words, I woke up
knowing I'd come back, stepped on
the familiar shores of life
where Death's feared, a distant distrustful thing.
My drowse burst like a glacier that cracks
from rumble of a seed of fire
that explodes somewhere
in earth's deep sleep.

Mules on the Tube

"And each man fixed his eyes before his feet..."
--T.S. Eliot

Mules on the tube
brown, black or blonde

with loads
of their sordid lives

on the weary lashes
of their vanquished eyes

swollen from centuries
of intent stare into the growling eyes of the lion kings

living on the margins
of a millionaire London's frugal Chalkfarms,

Cockfosters,
Edgwares and East Ends

chewing Tesco's vegpledges
having forgotten hungers of their homelands

barren querns, hollowed silos of plenty
starving hillsides and famished deltas of their continents

silent and stern
almost tongueless

learning to
shrug and be smug and grim and longfaced

mastering
sharp accents of bare survival

struggling to surf
on the invisibe silk roads of city's cyber alleys

moving like living ghosts
in long oblong grave-shaped bogies

of Central, City,
Circle or Picadilly lines

carrying packs of Pet A Manger Sandwitches,
Coca or Beck's cans, Tesco frosen foods,

Marks and Spencer cinamen rolls,
Mars chocobars and Sainsbury mangoes as home grown deities

wearing wires of ipods
straps of laptops, cyber mobiles and datedotcoms

as sureshot weapons of mass success

stoned from the ariel airs
of free Airtel or Orange 'talktimes'

wrapped up
in the Woolsworth warmth

of long fluffy coats, scented scarves,
monkey caps, rainbow sweaters imported from Asia

Poppies, paperbacks
and perfumes from Boots and Superdrugs

facing free copies of *Metro*
or *London Paper* like profound script of a prayer wheel

or dozing
like Lamas on a nightly vigil

or just awake from work
or weekends and parties on prairies

moving like emperors
of icecream on the power of the underground *Oysters*

from Totehamcourt Road to High Barnet
Waterloo Station to Battersea, Victoria Terminal to Brixton

risking raids from the imported tigers
of terror in the haven of human rights

forgetful of alarms
and scurity announcements

stalking the arched corridors
of an ashen underworld, lining up

dutifully on the floating stairways
like pilgrimages to their favorite shrines

packed like domestic fowls
in the early morning trains

bobbing like Barbie Dolls on weekends,
oblivious of the stare of the mighty Big Ben

stamping steps of the ancient
carriage routes like Supermen

clanging
steely stairways of ecscalators

mules on the tube
self-made slaves on the footsteps of prodigious Pound

men in a hurry
the third eye etenally on the Abbey of *A Hole in the Wall*

women with history
from the land of dogmas and dictators

men with degrees,
portfolios and myspace profiles

women with angles and arts
wide enough to make doors into heart's dark holes

on the run to build
a babylon of a fresh space on a new globe.

Shall I kiss your eyes ?

Kohl-eyed daughter
of Lorca, milky egret of Guadalquivir,

Mary of Mezquita,
Queen of Cordoba drunk from the scent

of orange flowers, lurid patios
lit from the glow of blood red geraniums

and history's glorious guilt,
shall I kiss your eyes?

Pearl of the Mediterranean,
blue umbrella of Andalusia enduring

endless inquisitions,
thousand rains and injured sun shines,

Rafael's own great
grand heiress born out from the confluence

of angular rivers bleeding
in the *duenda* of flamingo dancers,

shall I go on
my knees like a befallen moor,

a vanquished Caliph to serve
the keys of my smoldering city

to the chuckle of
of the winning Cardinal

and tear a morsel of sweet bread
baked in Aphrodite's own oven?

Kohl-eyed daughter
of Lorca, milky egret of Guadalquivir, ,

Mary of Mezquita,
Queen of Cordoba

shall I kiss your eyes?

Nine Asian Wives

When I finally came out
of St. Michael's underground station

I could hardly believe
she existed and actually waited for me.

When we circled Notre Dome
like Hindu devotees round a shrine

she kept remembering names
of the restaurants that served sexiest fish.

When we stood over
the bridge lost in Seine's splendor

she said she had had
four children from three husbands.

When I held her slender fingers
and stroked her cheekbones

she started guessing
age of my nine Asian wives.

When I lifted her red tresses
pricking mirrors of her green eyes

she kept worrying about my scarlet
scarf that the winds might take away.

When my fingers touched
tips of her damp water-well,

she muttered--
Do you have a sweet tongue?

When I used my roving hands
to silence the shudder of her deep lakes

she grabbed them
to calm the quivering doves of her slender body.

When at last we kissed
and saw surreal clouds in the French skies

drawing shapes
from the chapters of Kama Sutra,

she worried someone might
steal away my black bag lying unattended nearby.

When I whispered
the songs of the waves that surged in my soul

at each twitch of fish
in the river of our stitched mouths

she said she had to go
and get some euros from a cash machine nearby.

When we stood at the Point Zero
like perfect lovers holding our bodies

enraptured gospels of fresh faith,
she asked if I could later help carry

her groggy gas cylinder
up into her apartment on the seventh floor.

When in the end we parted
with a promise to meet again

and back in London,
I lifted my pen to write notes on the scandal

she sent me an email—

"Since you will leave soon
we better not meet.

Return safe home to
your hundred children from nine Asian wives..."

"At Forty You Die"

At forty two moons start throbbing
like bright eyes of your own children.
At forty two people you dream of
most frequently, two people who dreamt
of you and your eyes all their lives.

At forty in the early
dawn of your desperate decades
you start dreaming of your mother first.

She comes limping
like a wounded cockroach
from the other world
to clasp your sweaty palms
to kiss your eyebrows
withering under the blind stare
of a merciless sun,
to complains of the tulips that faded
under the blind stare of a merciless sun.

At forty you dream
of your father frequently,
a Buddha or an exhausted god,
a lion repentant for a lifetime,
a familiar stranger who made you
what you are in your dreams
and left you alone,
bleeding on the mule-paths of life.
At forty you see him everywhere,
in the creases of your skin,
in the puffed-out eyelids,
in the fluffy temples
where two crescent moons appear,
silvery and savage like ensuing life's itinerary.

At forty he lusts in the crazed
fields of your blood vessels.
He escorts you to
the open spaces of his cherished riverbanks
pavilions of tantric priests
ashrams of ascetics before bonfires of annihilation.
He guides you to the bog lands
of his fond memories where once
his beloved woman lived and
then left him, one by one,
"Forgot the old chums, fell in the trap of new ones"

She comes limping
like a wounded cockroach
from the other world
to clasp your sweaty palms
to kiss your eyebrows
withering under the blind stare
of a merciless sun
to complain of the tulips that faded
under the blind stare of a merciless sun.

At forty your own woman's mouth
starts smelling of deceit,
a Bhairab's mask,
a masculine leer along
the canyons of her body.

At forty you start
questioning questions
and decide to die
like one dies in poetry or books.
Or proverbs that proved false--
People above forty should be shot dead.

You resolve what you didn't all life long--
to reach out to touch

the rim of unheard horizons
elusive Shangri-la from where no return
to exquisite valleys of life is possible.

But your children's eyes start
shining like burning stars
along the moons of your secret lusts.

At forty you die to be born again
and again in the theatre of your children's eyes

PART THREE
Whitman's Daughter

St. Johns

The snow that crinkled beneath our feet,
feel of apple crumble in the mouth, the blue waters
sweet as the local wine,
the glacial winds that came into the Narrow
like the first few humble footsteps on the lord's own island,
then the figures, eyes sharp and piercing, savage tip of a Viking spear
a coffin ship narrowly escaping a dash against an iceberg.

Song of the snow that comes wetting
snout of a killer whale, the song of a dolphin
as she touches a human heart on island's shimmering edge,
"You can kiss me if you like,"
or "I have this strong temptation
to kiss you, but I think it's inappropriate at this moment..."

Song of the alpine firs and birch and sycamore,
her thigh bright birch trunks,
the native harp in-between playing
to raging ballad of the mighty moose ravishing a lover,
majestic hubris of the frozen river
melting into a fresh avatar of an aroused Shiva Sea.

In the looking glass, shaped like Europe's crusty map,
the town ogles the face it sees. The Duke's Bar,
warm from his the travels in the strange lands:
"First I broke my left arm
and after two weeks I broke my broken arm again."

The knight of the town of blue-eyed,
green-eyed, hazel eyed nymphs
a family of mermaids turning
white silence into turquoise lakes,
a colony of salmon and cod, lobster and languid sleep.

A little girl waits in the glassy window, a meditating cat
looking at an unknown anonymous strange man,
a lover she would have when she grows up.

The Duke's Bar warmed from his guests and gossip
"On New Year Eve, I was about
to shut my office, but she came up the stairs
clad in a fur coat only, and said,
"Here's your present, come and take it."

Cleveland

Tears in the eyes
of the lake Erie have frozen,
hidden in its eye sockets
the thirst of the world's fresh waters.

Its waves grey
like Gandhi's feeble staff
as he raises his neck
in rusting belt's cold furnaces,
rolling mills and withered gardens.

The vacant eyes
of the church staring into
the glassy surface of the skyscrapers
that once wrote the billionaire future of the city of steel.

The cartoon of a corrupt politician
eating with his horse's bushy tail
and the freedom stamp silently tilted sideways,
ready to move over to some obscure edge of history.

The town where Anne Sexton
came to declare her resolution to 'do' it.
I met a deer there,
probably her current incarnation,

and in the cemetery of the famous dead
a raccoon that came hunting for crumbs,
in fashion of the town itself making a living
out of service to the aged and the ailing

Like the pear blossoms
the deer had dared to come out

to greet the spring from Hart Crane's bridge
where he once waited to kiss his cruel mistress, the Sea.

Your fingers

Supple as velvet
body of a laughing thrush
lush as notes
from a Himalayan flute

alive and angular
the birds of paradise
in the grim underworld
of the mad metropolis

a feel of your face,
preface to your body's
scented water wells
that I long to touch
with my naked lips

a fish that wd throb
in the streams
of my blood vessels
manufactured from god's
own omniscient heart-mind
later cursed and maligned
from the shame of falling
in love with his own daughter

long and soft
tendrils of a long lost sleep
wisp of the marble
limbed goddesses sculpted
by saints in the dark caves

in stale and smothered airs
of the NYC subway,
grim as a graveyard,

your fingers in my hands
a miracle
from the goddess
of the winds of the world.

Twisted Muse

1

Cindy

She took offense
when I touched her

in every breath her husband
in every sentence a history

of her happy conjugal life
in the wilderness of the Grand Canyon.

Her painted chin
had a grey hair protruding

like a spike
in Adam's glistening apple

When I grabbed
sleeping dragon s of her broad

bow shaped shoulders
accidently touching smoldering

plume of her widowed breaths
she shrank into shrimp

and vanished
on the shores of the Pacific Ocean.

2

Living Waters

I've learnt to say
no recently, she confided
as a way of revelation to me,
offering a glistening apple
after a car wash at the gas station.
Her shoulders shone
like cheekbones of the sleeping Indian rising above us.
I looked at her marble shoulders
and touched them, the flowers
in the boulevards of Boulder downtown
laughed hysterically. She played
a cassette of transatlantic music
laced with devotional Tabla beats
as we drove through the clean Boulder air.
One more time I leaned
and kissed the crown of her body,
daggers of pure steel
erect in my heart, bow of Frida Kahlo's hunter,
"I've learnt to water
my love in the name of the Lord,"
she squealed, almost in divine anguish,
"I've learnt to seek compassion
in the waters of His mercy,
I've learnt to say
no to things earthly."

"I'm the living water," I felt like quoting
the Book of Revelations to her.
And, it has to flow on.

Manhattan Beach, LA

Flower faced beach town
whose distances my steps can't measure.
Cars race over its petals
with the fury of a sea's muscular power
tirelessly kissing its belly button
shining its nude skin
from the surf of its blue waters.

Huge baby shark that Pedro holds
uncouthly up in the air is what
a roadside juggler would do to a sloth bear

or a monkey trapped for a life time back home.

"I'll put it back again," I hear him say
to his crowd, and actually see him put it
back into the icebox to prove his claim.

There are stains of blood
beside the box, bruises
from constantly pulling it by the tail
for a graceless display. I see eyes of a huge
baby shark, pale and shame-ridden, panting.

"I'll throw it back into the waters of course,
No, no, I am not going to eat it," he laughs,
and clicks his slithering tongue. "After a week or so,
you see it will go down the drain
of the lighthouse, back into the sea."

Song of the small stalls

In the Amstel train
I missed them the most,
mutilated multitudes on the jolting wheels of life.

It was Buffalo, Rochester, Syracuse
or some such town
and as train stopped I woke up abruptly,
thinking I've arrived at some Indian station--
Panipat, Gonda or Kanpur.

For a moment it appeared
they wd swarm in like houseflies,
buzzing names of their meager merchandise,
for a moment it seemed
they wd rush in the classy Amstel compartment
to share my American solitude--

Bare-backed boy sweeping
the littered floor of the train
with the makeshift broom of his ragged shirt.
The blind beggar with a gnarled arm
shouting Kabir songs, his grandson
a fragile staff on the dark trail of his life.
Children in circus costumes,
mock mustaches, motley caps with piggy tails,
the sister passing through steel rings
her adolescent bones creaking
like bamboo-posts of countryside string cots.

Sunken cheeked scrawny widow
selling socks and bangles
and later in the night herself.
Men carrying deep wicker baskets
full of papad, or steel buckets topped

with salted peanuts or boiled grams piles
tinged with lemon or red chilies.

Robust hill girls in scarlet shawls begging,
with the authority of roving priests,
the permit of fierce
brass goddesses in their vermilion splattered trays

Or young women of long black braids
throwing faded little cards
printed in bad English pleading
attention to rescue them
from a recent catastrophe.

Eunuchs of lusty nose rings clapping,
touching your groin in a special peck,
a glint of mischief in their starry eyes,

Chai vendors, their throaty cry
piercing silence of the night stations,

small stalls
on the wheels of hunger

tiny supermarkets
on the wavering watercourse of life...

But no one came
as the train stood in utter silence
in an almost empty stations,
no one moved, talked,
smiled or even broke into a helpless cry.

Slowly the train moved on
and I saw juniper trees
lined up along the tracks
each branch loaded from fresh snow,

mere beggars with multiple hands.

Through the glassy panes
of the overheated compartment
beyond sprawling vistas
of snow and light I caught
sight of a dozen ravens
by the edge of a frozen pond, sitting
as if busy in a corporate meeting,
a feel of having at last
conquered a long war
over the mutilated multitudes.

Latino Love

Latino love found me
in a bustling NYC party accidently

Latino love took me
to be a shaman, for sure

my black bag bulging
from magical rainbows,

serpents from a Hindu Heaven,
skull of an abducted female Yeti,

magic mushrooms,
Yarchagumba and other Himalayan aphrodisiacs

to raise even
a stodgy stone from its Amazon sleep.

Latino love adored
my pagan adulation of her long brown legs,

golden limbed goddess
inside her spacious body's wide sanctuary

Latino love wished to
make love to me all night long,

translating my works
except love poems into Spanish

Latino love wanted
to rent my brown body, turn it

into a sacred sutra,
a sufi song or a shatoosh shawl

to wrap around her shoulders
all the time in all West Village parties

Latino love said
she understood sanguine silence of my snow peaks

Latino love
wanted some action right away,

flowers of wild passions wet
from her impassioned breaths

"Can you read my future,"she asked,
spreading her palms after the waves had receded,

"Maybe there's a Juju
in the spidery maze of these heavenly alleys."

Latino love
wanted to be a wife I already had.

Your Name

Your name
like your yogurt kisses

I long to forget
in the boulevards of NYC's alphabet avenues

Your kisses
like your cherry mouth

sings Starbucks songs
of winds stirred by flames of freedom.

Your mouth
like your sleek tongue

licks sadness
out of my life's numbered streets.

Your tongue
like your jasmine breath

knows scent
of secret Amazons and seashores.

Your breath
like your floral smiles

sparks of delight
in the moldy days of my remaining life.

Your smile
like your bright eyes

stays calm as stars
over blue Atlantic waters.

Your eyes
like your dolphin heart

beats frantic
in the numbered streets of Manhattan.

Your heart mind
reading horoscopes

of my life's withered leaf
aflutter in the dark streets of your city.

NYC Poem

Lonely lunch hour
at Whole Food Market,
Union Square. Gandhi with his humble stick
amidst blooming flowers
rising by weekly organic food stalls,
Farms Inc, Van Houston, Veggies Barn
by the Staples and Star Bucks Store.
American flags furling
in the dappled summer skies
above Empire State Building.
Eat, Shop, Visit, Green Market,
the banner printed from the flowers,
yellow, red, maroon, blue ,
furling from a lamppost above NYC city bus.
Italian ties, $5 each, or 5 for $ 20,
Designer sunglasses made in Asia.
The teenage girl opposite me
eating her sandwich with classic Krinkle chips,
a glistening apple put by her tray,
her hair done in multiple braids
sewn with rings from the colors of America
and like my own daughter
the food she spills over her dress...
The blond girl by my side reading
a French comedy, facing the steel framed
pictures from Kathmandu's Asan vegetable bazaar
or Daryaganj's fruit market.
Chinese girl by the grassy window
overlooking a Tibetan demonstration
against Olympics in the square below
speaking English with a shrill NYC accent,
a paperback of *Eat, Pray, Love* in her hand.
And the black woman's headgear
like Buddha's caterpillar cap,

hurling me into the depths of the world
left behind, in a hurry,
Rahul, Yashodhara, Brikuti, Lumbini.
I pick up my mobile and ring back home
to wake my kids round the heated globe.
It must be midnight now,
"My Pop, he's crazy,"
my ten-year-old son would say,
smiling happily in his sleep.
I miss him here in American food market
tinged with spices of Asia,
miles away as he sleeps
to wake up to the sheen of eternal Himalayan snow...

Luna, fish on Long Island Sound

It sent a shudder
through my body, your wilderness,
your volcanic eruptions,
your history of shaking colossal shapes
and shining like a magical mirror.
Salt of your long sleek tongue
hit the milky reservoir of my heart,
an Indian hunter's spear. Huntington,
Port Jefferson, New Heaven, Southampton.
Sea sang names of my forgotten ancestors,
savage rise of the half moon
on the haven of seashells, the Devil's belt.
Smug faced Dutch share broker
by my side on the Expressway
cracked open like a shell
and turned into a chattering elf
as we entered your body.
You stood by my side,
your body bare, almost,
your white hand on my shoulder
and turned into all the fish of the Sound—
blue fish, striped bass, winter flounder,
Atlantic salmon, fluke, butter fish.
I picked up wavering tide
of your breath and strung a mantra out of it
in the clean sky of my lung's pagodas.
A black bird like Anne Sexton
crossing the estuary sang a dark song.
Fine, fine, you added, fine!
your breasts visible, a visitor
to the land of mother glaciers
where once a lonely soul eked out
a living by sorting slippery stones
and threading a song of Self,

away from many a Manhattans.
Fine, fine, baby, came the voice,
your big lips on my mouth,
you have finally reached home
you dreamt centuries ago
in the raging rainbow of your rocking embryo.

Whitman's Daughter

"I've never seen anyone
as sweet smelling as this girl," I told George.

It was raining outside
when I first saw her in the barn, Huntington,
Walt Whitman's birthplace on the long islands,
the udders of Lord Krishna's cows
that he squeezed to fill his shiny buckets
full with milk, honey and moonlight
bruised lust and lethal longing
spilling into the cosmic mouth
wherein galaxies multiplied
in long sleek blades of his catalogues
throbbing like salmon
in the sweet waters of the Cold Spring Harbor.

Yes, it was raining when
I again saw her in the crowded barn looking bar
and next moment found myself up close
as my withering skin to my soul.
Lilacs bloomed outside and a small wooden cradle
rocked by an empty bed in his house
an endless count of the racing hours of my youth.

"I've never seen anyone as sweet smelling as this girl,"
I leaned over and told George "A perennial tree.
This must be Whitman's own daughter."

Right then she turned around,
and faced me and introduced herself,
"Hey, I know you!
Weren't we in the same train this evening?
I saw you there. Remember,
I was standing near the entrance door,
In fact, I was rushing to come to this bar.
What are you doing here?"

New Found Land

A loose moose
on a strip of snow

a Himalayan landscape
of junipers and pines along permanent snowline

a mini-snow kingdom
sans altitude, vertigo, hunger

and fatal ascents
up the sordid slopes of karma.

The mountains on the island,
mere pimples on a white woman's sparkling face.

Yak would
find a friend here

So would Yeti
a lover for a lifetime

and dance
on the frozen ponds

singing songs
of eternal icebergs and endless snow.

About the Poet

Recipient of fellowships and grants from The Rockefeller Foundation, Ireland Literature Exchange, Trubar Foundation, Slovenia, The Institute for the Translation of Hebrew Literature and The Foundation for the Production and Translation of Dutch Literature, **Yuyutsu RD Sharma** is a distinguished poet and translator.

He has published nine poetry collections including, *Milarepa's Bones, 33 New Poems,* (Nirala, New Delhi 2012), *Nepal Trilogy, Photographs and Poetry on Annapurna, Everest, Helambu & Langtang* (www.Nepal-Trilogy.de, Epsilonmedia, Karlsruhe, 2010), a 900-page book with renowned German photographer, Andreas Stimm, *Space Cake, Amsterdam, & Other Poems from Europe and America,* (2009, Indian reprint 2014) and *Annapurna Poems,* 2008), Reprint, 2012, 14).

Yuyutsu has also brought out a translation of Irish poet Cathal O' Searcaigh poetry in Nepali in a bilingual collection entitled, *Kathmandu: Poems, Selected and New* (2006) and a translation of Hebrew poet Ronny Someck's poetry in Nepali in a bilingual edition, *Baghdad, February 1991 & Other Poems.* He has translated and edited several anthologies of contemporary Nepali poetry in English and launched a literary movement, *Kathya Kayakalpa* (Content Metamorphosis) in Nepali poetry.

Two books of his poetry, *Poemes de l' Himalayas* (L'Harmattan, Paris) and *Poemas de Los Himalayas* (Cosmopoeticia, Cordoba, Spain) have appeared in French and Spanish respectively.

Widely traveled author, he has read his works at several prestigious places including The Poetry Café, London, The Seamus Heaney Center for Poetry, Belfast, New York University, New York, The Kring, Amsterdam, P.E.N, Paris, Knox College, Illinois, Whittier College, California, Baruch College, New York, WB Yeats' Center, Sligo, Gustav Stressemann Institute, Bonn, Rubin Museum, New York, Irish Writers' Centre, Dublin, The Guardian Newsroom, London, Trois Rivieres Poetry Festival, Quebec, Arnofini, Bristol, Borders, London, Slovenian Book Days, Ljubljana, Royal Society of Dramatic Arts, London, Gunter Grass House, Bremen, Nehru Center, London, March Hare, Newfoundland, Canada, South Bank Center, London, Gannon University, Erie, Frankfurt Book Fair, Frankfurt, Indian International Center, New Delhi, and Villa Serbelloni, Italy.

He has held workshops in creative writing and translation at Queen's University, Belfast, University of Ottawa and South Asian Institute, Heidelberg University, Germany, University of California, Davis,

Sacramento State University, California and New York University, New York.

Yuyutsu's own work has been translated into German, French, Italian, Slovenian, Hebrew, Spanish and Dutch. He has also published his non-fiction, *Annapurnas & Stains of Blood: Life, Travel and Writing a Page of Snow* and edits *Pratik, A Magazine of Contemporary Writing*. He contributes literary columns to Nepal's leading daily, *The Himalayan Times*.

Yuyutsu was at the Poetry Parnassus Festival organized to celebrate London Olympics 2012 where he represented Nepal and India. He will visit NYU later this year as Special Visiting Poet and in 2014, Nicaragua as Guest Poet to participate in International Poetry Festival of Granada.

Half the year, he travels and reads all over the world from his works and conducts creative writing workshop at various universities in North America and Europe but goes trekking in the Himalayas when back home.

Books by Yuyutsu RD Sharma

POETRY

A Prayer in Daylight (Poems), 1984

Hunger of our Huddled Huts & other Poems, 1989

Some Female Yeti & other Poems, 1995

The Lake Fewa and a Horse, Poems New, 2005

www.AroundAnnapurna.de: A photographic and Poetic Journey around Annapurnas, Nepal

www.WayToEverest.de:A photographic and Poetic Journey to the Foot of Everest, 2006

Annapurna Poems, 2008

Everest Failures, 2008

Space Cake Amsterdam & Other Poems of Europe and America

Milarepa's Bone, Helambu

Poemes de l' Himalayas (French)

Poemas de Los Himalayas (Spanish)

FICTION & NON-FCITION

Annapurnas and Stains of Blood (Travelogue), 2009

TRANSLATIONS

Dying in Rajasthan, 1985
Short Stories by Ramanand Rathi
(Translated from the Rajasthan)

Folk Tales of Sherpa & Yeti, 2008
Shiva Dhakal
(Translated from the Nepali)

Roaring Recitals: Five Nepali Poets,
(Gopal Prasad Rimal, Bhupi Sherchan & Others)
(Translated from the Nepali)

Kathmandu
Poems Selected and New (An English/Nepali Bilingual Edition)
Cathal O' Searcaigh
Translated from the Gaelic by Seamus Heaney, John Montague and others
Translated into the Nepali

EDITED

Elysium in the Halls of Hell, 1991
Poems about India by David Ray

Dispossessed Nests: The 1984 Poems, 1986
By Jayanta Mahapatra

Bagar: An Asian Poetry Special Number, *(1989-90) Kathmandu, Nepal*

General Editor, Nirala Series *(Since 1989)*

Guest Editor, Omega, *Special Issue on Nepali Poetry (www.howlingdogpress.com)*
with Michael Annis, Howling Dog Press

Pratik: *A Magazine of Contemporary Writing, since 1990*

Pratik's Special Dutch issue *(2007 Spring Issue)*
with Harry Zevenbergen as Guest Editor

Pratik's Special British issue *(2007 Summer Fall Issue)*
with Pascale Petit as Guest Editor

Nirala Series

A Series of Contemporary Writing

Nine New York Poems: A Prelude
To A Blizzard In My Bones: New York Poems
Yuyutsu RD Sharma
ISBN-81-8250-032-X 2012 Hard pp.64

Space Cake, Amsterdam
& Other Poems from Europe and America
Yuyutsu RD Sharma
ISBN-81-8250-059-1 2014 Hard pp. 110

Pez / Fish
A Bilingual Edition
Mariela Dreyfus
Translated from the Spanish by E.M. O'Connor
ISBN-81-8250-055-9 2012 Hard pp.64

Milarepa's Bones, Helambu
33 New Poems
Yuyutsu RD Sharma
ISBN-81-8250-032-X 2012 Hard pp.64

Garuda
& Other Astral Poems
David B. Austell
ISBN-81-8250-038-9 2012 Hard pp.72

Inside Out, Upside Down,
& Round and Round
Poems Selected & New
John J. Trause
ISBN-81-8250-049-4 2012 Paper pp.83

All the way from Kathmandu
Selected Jazz Poems
John Clarke
ISBN-81-8250-042-7 2012 Paper pp.82

No Child More Perfect & Other Poems
Christi Shannon Kline
ISBN-81-8250-039-7 2012 Paper pp.82

Things Missed in Exile
New Poems
E. Avi Frishman
ISBN-81-8250-029-X 2012 Paper pp. 49

Journey Though India and Nepal
Poems/Pictures
Robert Scotto & Lu Wu
ISBN-81-8250-045-1 2012 Hard pp.84

Incident on the Orient
Poems by
George Wallace
ISBN-81-8250-044-3 2012 Paper pp. 76

Little Creek & Other Poems
David Austell
ISBN 81-8250- 031-1 2011 Hard pp.200 Rs.495

Lizard Licking, Donegal & Other Poems
Diane Hamilton
ISBN - 81-81-8250-033-8 2011 Paper Rs. 295

The Price of Heaven
Travel Stories from India and Nepal
Evald Flisar
Translated from Slovene by the Author & Alan McConnell-Duff
ISBN 81-8250- 020-6 2009 Paper pp.140 Rs. 195

Annapurna Poems
Poems New and Selected
Yuyutsu RD Sharma
ISBN 81-8250-013-5 2008 Hard pp.150 Rs. 295

Baghdad, February 1991
&Other Poems
Ronny Someck
Translated into Nepali by Yuyutsu RD Sharma
ISBN 81-8250- 018-4 2009 Hard pp.200 Rs. 250

After Tagore
Poems Inspired by Rabindranath Tagore
David Ray
ISBN 81-8250-007-9 2007 Hard pp. 115 Rs. 295

Hunger of Our Huddled Huts
& Other Poems
Yuyutsu R.D.
ISBN 81-85693-80-3 2007 pp.65 Rs. 95

Kathmandu
Poems Selected and New (An English/Nepali Bilingual Edition)
Cathal O Searcaigh
Translated from the Gaelic by Seamus Heaney,
John Montague and others
Translated into the Nepali by Yuyutsu R.D. Sharma
ISBN 81-8250-006-0 2006 Hard pp. 105 Rs. 250

The Lake Fewa & a Horse
Poems New
Yuyutsu R.D. Sharma
ISBN 81-85693-34-X 2005 Paper pp. 108 Rs. 125

Muna Madan
A Play in the Jhyaure Folk Tradition
Laxmi P. Devkota
Translated from the Nepali by Anand P. Shrestha
ISBN 81-85693-94-3 2000 pp.65 Rs. 85

Fever (Short Stories)
Sita Pandey
Translated from the Nepali
ISBN 81-85693-93-5 2001 Paper pp.96 Rs. 95

Says Meera
An Anthology of Devotional Songs of Meera,
India's Greatest Woman Poet
Translated from the Hindi by Vijay Munshi
ISBN 81-85693-96-X 2001 Paper pp.76 Rs. 195

Some Female Yeti & other Poems
Yuyutsu R.D.
ISBN 81-8250-010-9 2007 pp.68 Rs. 95

In the City of Partridges (Poems)
Jagdish Chatturvedi
ISBN 81-85693-99-4 2004 Paper pp.90 Rs. 95

Roaring Recitals: Five Nepali Poets
Gopal Prasad Rimal, Bhupi Sherchan, Shailendra & Others
Translated from the Nepali by
Yuyutsu R.D. Sharma
ISBN 81-85693-95-1 1999 Hard pp.99 Rs. 150

Summer Rain
Three Decades of Poetry
K. Satchidanandan
ISBN 81-85693-90-0 1995 Paper pp.188 Rs. 150

Sheet of Snow
An Anthology of Stories from the Himalayas
Translated from the Nepali by Nagendra Sharma
ISBN 81-85693-61-7 1997 paper pp.125 Rs. 95

Dispossessed Nests: The 1984 Poems
Jayanta Mahapatra
ISBN 81-85693-74-9 1986 pp.69 Paper Rs. 15

To the Battlefield on an Elephant
Columns of Fire
Tara Nath Sharma
ISBN 81-85693-44-7 1999 pp.164 paper Rs. 195

The Change
A Novel based on the 1990 Democratic Upsurge in Nepal
Rishikeshab Raj Regmi
ISBN 81-85693-62-5 2001 pp.125 Rs. 95

Blackout (A Novel)
Tara Nath Sharma
Translated from the Nepali by Larry Hartsell
ISBN 81-85693-82-X 1990 pp.122 Rs. 100

Elysium in the Halls of Hell
Poems about India David Ray
ISBN 81-85693-84-6 1991 pp.160 Rs. 125

A Prayer in Daylight (Poems)
Yuyutsu R.D.
ISBN 81-85693-72-2 1984 paper pp.68 Rs. 95

Dying in Rajasthan (Short Stories)
Ramanand Rathi
ISBN 81-85693-71-4 1985 pp.62 Rs. 95